6-Week Cycles

Boost your team's morale and productivity through clearer project direction, improved communication, and regularly scheduled breaks. This book takes you through my team's step-by-step process on how we implemented Basecamp's idea of 6-week cycles over the last 3 years.

This book is dedicated to my incredible parents who showed me what it was to gamble on your dreams and turn them into reality.

table of
contents

1 6-WEEK CYCLES ARE JUST PLANNING

2 MONEY ISN'T THE MOTIVATOR

3 HOW TO USE 6-WEEK CYCLES

4 LIST OUT EVERYTHING YOU NEED TO DO

5 THE "AND THEN...?" GAME

6   PLAN FOR EACH DAY

7   CHECK-IN & CHECK-OUT MEETINGS

8   CYCLE SHEET EXTRAS

9   A KEYSTONE HABIT

10   6-WEEK CYCLES ARE NOT THE ANSWER

Foreword

While this book is a step-by-step framework for working in 6-Week Cycles, it's ultimately about respecting time. I was at a business skill-building workshop on time management when the coordinator asked, "when someone is on their deathbed and you ask if they'd like to have more time or more money, which one do you think they'd pick?"

First off, holy shit! What a thing to drop on a room full of business people. Second…more time, obviously.

And "obviously" because we know this! We know we are supposed to value every moment. We're reminded of it when someone close to us passes away, but then we slip back into the same routines. In the same way we already know the benefits of meditation, eating better, not smoking, and cherishing the small things in life, we just…don't do it. Usually because, "we don't have time."

We have time. But we think we don't.
Which, makes time itself an interesting concept and also our enemy.

Would you volunteer at a local organization to help those less fortunate than you? Sure — if you had the time.
Would you spend more time with the people you love in your life? Sure — but only if you had more time.
Would you actually go to the gym and start cooking more? Of course…if there was time.

Time. Time! TIME.

It's always about time. I consider time our enemy when it prevents us from fulfilling our intentions. And while we live in a time based society, this enemy had to have come from somewhere. So I did the dirty work and tracked it down. I chased time all the way back to 1657, and it's there I found something incredible. The invention of the balance spring.

This little invention made perpetual motion possible. By attaching some cogs and rotor, this simple device made the measurement of time possible.

Once we had the ability to measure time, we started measuring every-thing. We could find out how fast something moved by understanding how far it went over X amount of time. We could track moments in a day. And eventually, we learned we could measure human performance.

Go to school for X amount of time.
Then, go to college for X amount of time.
After that, you're qualified to sit at this desk for X amount of time per day, 5 days a week, with X amount of time off per year.
Yay!

What an insane metric to use! Yet you, your parents, your grandparents, your great-grandparents, and so on, have lived in a society constructed around time.

Still today, in our technologically advanced society, we allow this broken metric to serve as the backbone to too many business models. You're expected to sacrifice X amount of time per day in exchange for X dollars per year.

Time for money. The one thing we know we can't ever create more of, we frivolously trade away.

Same thing humans do with any resource we have in abundance, we exploit it. We give it away freely. We take it for granted and are sometimes blind to the amazing gift of life we've been given.

"If you have the opportunity to play this game of life, you need to appreciate every moment. A lot of people don't appreciate their moment until it's passed."

- Kanye West

I know, I just quoted Kanye in a business book; but what can I say? I'm a Ye fan. And in this case, he's right. We don't appreciate it. We hear people say things like, "same shit, different day". We'll go through an entire week just waiting for the weekend instead of realizing we have the opportunity to make a difference every day.

Every.
Damn.
Day.

If only, we had the time.

My hope is this book helps you find time in your own life. Hell, I even kept the book short so you don't have to spend a lot of time reading it. Take what's here. Find out what works for you. Make a difference in the lives of your children, your family, and your community. We're living in a world that needs that right now.

01

6-Week Cycles
are just planning

" It required minimal effort and
yielded a much greater reward."

Don't be fooled! Seriously, you can stop reading right now. The whole point of this is to simply plan for 6 weeks of work. But then, you need to actually do it.

All I did was take a concept I heard from Jason Fried, blend it with ideas from other thought leaders like Robert Cialdini, Charles Duhigg, Momoko Price, Casey Clark, Angela Vitzthum, Mig Reyes, Clayton Christensen, Oren Klaff, and others, and added my experience running a creative agency. From there it was combined principles in conversion-rate optimization, working with clients, and building a digital product company. Put all that together, and we arrive at this book.

What I found, however — that's big. It started to feel like the kind of stuff that could really change lives. Even better is that it required minimal effort and yielded a much greater reward — the true millennial way.

And if it changes lives, maybe it can change communities.
I feel if more people are involved in their communities, it starts to shape cities.

From cities to states and states to countries.
That maybe, maybe, there's a chance to make some real change happen in this world of ours with something as simple as a differently structured work environment. I will admit, I tend to take things to a grandiose scale. I'm a dreamer! But, this just feels like a better way to work.

Even if it doesn't have this giant effect on the world, it still helps:
• Set higher expectations
• Better understand our capabilities
• Increase productivity
• Create a strong, innovative work culture

This idea came from Basecamp

First off, thank you to Jason Fried. If it weren't for his constant questioning of the corporate world and experimentation with work environments at his own company, others like myself may not have been as inspired to realize things can be different.

Launched in 2004, and also from Chicago, Basecamp was an easy-to-use and purposefully designed project management system. As it gained popularity, so did its CEO, Jason Fried. His Ted Talk about "why work doesn't happen at work" presented some pretty amazing ideas, and his books have continued to push for new workplace methodologies.

In speaking with one of Basecamp's sales people I was invited to a presentation at Basecamp's offices. The topic — how Basecamp uses Basecamp to build Basecamp.

I was one of 20 people who attended the presentation. During it, Jason emphasized the idea of breathing room in a working environment. He and his team had toyed with different methodologies to find breathing room and finally settled on one that worked best for them. Their preferred method? Take 2 weeks to plan the next 6 weeks of work.

What the $&%#? You can do that?!
If I plan out everything I am going to work on for 6 weeks, I can take it easy for 2 weeks?

I loved this! And I did that thing where you start daydreaming as soon as you hear an idea. Your mind just starts racing with, "if I did this, I could do this. Then this could happen. THEN, I can do this!" I almost ran out of the room. I took the idea home with me and immediately started to look for ways I could implement this with my team.

I was running a creative agency at the time and had seven people working for me. I've always been of the mindset — if I want something for myself, the rest of my team should also have it. So, if I want to work this way, the whole team needs to work this way.

We began using 6-week cycles in April 2016. In 2018, we brought these cycles to a 20+ person team with employees in four different countries. Since then, the changes we've seen in productivity and communication have been amazing!

In this book, I will share what I have learned. All I knew of these cycles was Jason's idea of 6-on, 2-off. From there, I continued to mold the idea until it worked for my team. Incorporating spreadsheets, meetings, and combining it with concepts from sales, marketing, conversion-based copywriting, design, psychology, CRO, time management, social media, and a shit-ton of trial, error, and downright failure.

Jason, thank you for the inspiration and for your efforts in pushing for better workplace cultures. I hope this book helps drive those ideals further with those who read it. Things don't have to be the way they've always been.

02

Money isn't the Motivator

"Our capitalistic society has driven parents to spend more time working and less time with their families."

As a marketing consultant, I've worked with companies on a simple concept — what should I charge?

What I've learned is that it doesn't come down to a dollar amount. It's about the value of the goods/service the person is receiving.

Take beer for example. If I were to visit Northside Bar in Wicker Park on a Wednesday night at 10pm for their open mic, a beer is going to cost me $6. If I visit that same bar tomorrow at 5pm, that same beer would only cost me $4. But then, if I try to buy that same beer at Wrigley Field, it's $12.

Money has value because we put value in money as a society. As Philip Morgan points out in The Positioning Guide for Technical Firms, all value is perceived value. For the millennial generation, they've realized what P. Diddy tried to tell the world oh so many years ago about the trials and tribulations of having "mo money."

It's all perspective. It's also relative.

Make more and you'll probably spend more on bullshit. Make less and you might actually budget better.

But time — time can't be purchased. However, there is a way to help people manage their time more effectively.

By restructuring the work environment for efficiency, we can have more time. Maybe it's spending the day at home building a lego millennium falcon, taking a trip somewhere, or taking your kid out of school for the day. In creating a results-oriented environment we reward individuals for working hard.

And that, *that* has value. A type of value people are willing to work hard towards and want to be a part of.

A Focus on family

Somewhere along the line, we began downplaying the importance of raising children. To me, this serves as a contributing factor to the problems we see with mental health in America. Society has driven parents to spend more time working and less time with their families. More time at work, less time in their community.

Too many times I've heard about how expensive daycare is and the parents who work extra hard to pay for it. This feels wrong. Parents spend time away from their children, to make money, to pay for someone else to spend time with their child?! Holy shit. I can't be the only one who thinks this is ridiculous.

One day, my web developer, Aaron, had finished a project at 3pm. When I realized I had nothing for him to do, I scrambled to find stuff to fill up his last two hours. And why wouldn't I? I was paying Aaron to be there until 5pm, I should be getting every dollar I can out of him.

And then I stopped.

I asked myself, what I was doing with Aaron's time that was more important than him spending time with his children? Giving him little crap projects because he needed to stay until 5pm, just so he could drive home in traffic at the same time as everybody else? Taking even longer for him to see his family.

Felt like a jerk move on my part.

If I was asking Aaron to spend time away from his newborn daughter to be working for me, I'd better be damn sure his time is being spent effectively. To do that, I needed to be more prepared. I needed to know specifically which tasks I needed Aaron to complete so I could continue to do my job.

While I'm still looking for that person to spend my life with and start a family, when I get there, I refuse to not be an active part of my child's everyday life. And if I want that for myself, I want it for my team.

Be Results Oriented

"Too much stuff comes up during the week. We can't plan ahead."
- everybody, everywhere

Organizations often fall victim to the "too much stuff comes up" mentality. Employees just get through the day the best they can, and leave their job unhappy and uninspired. My fear is workers begin to think the smallest tasks are too big; therefore, change isn't possible. I'm further afraid this mindset gets brought home and instilled into their children. And for people to think, "things are too big, you cannot change them" feels like an incredibly incorrect and dangerous view of the world.

I already told you, I'm a dreamer. I would love to know what the world looks like when parents come home feeling accomplished at the end of each week. When they're excited to take on projects and set new goals because they realize achieving those goals *is* possible.

To me, a results-oriented work environment functions the same as value-based pricing. To be effective, we need to understand the value of what each employee can accomplish, as opposed to a set hourly rate for X amount of time.

At most jobs, what is your reward for finishing your work early? Was it more work?! *Ughhh!* That's so messed up.

Instead of encouraging a person to work more effectively, companies drain motivation. They train people to function at a lesser level because, well, there is no benefit for them to excel at their job.

Just the same. consistent. paycheck. every. time.

The next time you find yourself in a Lyft or Uber, ask the driver why they enjoy driving. When I ask that question, the answer is the same 9 out of 10 times — they love the flexibility. They work when and how much they want. It allows them to feel like their own boss while working for someone else.

It makes sense, too.

They know exactly what they need to get done.

Lyft/Uber doesn't say, "drive around from 9am to 5pm". They say, "you will make X if you do X rides." It's simple, and I believe ride-share drivers actually understand more about their upcoming work schedule than a majority of the working world.

What I've seen with my team

COGNITIVE CLOSURE

Entrepreneurs can empathize with the feeling of never being done. Work is rarely "over" by the end of a day, a week, a quarter, or even a fiscal year. When you finish one thing, great! Here is a list of 1,000 more things which still need to be finished.

With 6-week cycles, my team feels accomplished. Our mentality has shifted. It's not about getting through the thousand of things that need to be done, it's about completing the tasks we've planned to move the organization forward right now.

EXPECTATIONS ARE CLEAR

In the same way a Lyft driver knows exactly how many rides they need to give that week, my team has a clear understanding of what is expected from them. If something comes up during the week that prevents them from completing their tasks, that's fine! Because we already have future meetings planned, they just need to make sure their work is done by the next meeting.

It's not about how much time they put toward a task, it's whether or not the task is completed. If they're missing deadlines, the problem is you have an employee missing deadlines - or - you have a manager setting unrealistic expectations. In either case, 6-week cycles makes this easier to uncover, address, and correct.

WE ARE ALL LESS STRESSED

Regular meetings "on-cycle" has given my team a place to vent. A check out meeting at the end of each week lets them talk about the things which frustrate them, instead of letting it boil over and affect their performance. These meetings also prevent me from dropping random tasks on my team in the middle of the week. My team is respectful of their time, which causes me to be respectful of their time as well.

In the past, I absorbed work. If I had 10 things on my to do list one week, and my boss added 5 more on Tuesday, I would bust my ass to complete the tasks by Friday. But for what? My bosses didn't know I was overloaded because I didn't tell them I was overloaded, I worked extra to get everything done.

Every time I took on extra work, I allowed the problem to continue. I felt like I was working really hard, but nobody noticed — it's because they didn't. How could they?

To them, they'd simply see that it worked. They had their own things to worry about. I just...did it. And next time, they assumed they could do the same thing...and again....and again. Until suddenly, it becomes the new standard.

That was on me. I needed to celebrate my wins if I expected anyone else to celebrate them. I needed to take a Kanye style approach to letting my superiors know why I was incredible at my job.

Looking back, I can see how my superiors didn't understand how much work I had on my plate because I didn't speak up. I didn't respect my own time. When the extra work was dropped on me, I should have simply said "I can't complete these additional tasks this week, but I can have them for you by next Friday."

I recently went through a similar situation with the CEO of an organization my team works with. He didn't understand the value or impact of my employees because I wasn't selling their wins to him. As the director of the department, he only heard what we accomplished as a whole, and not the individual achievements.

It was up to me to sell their wins to the CEO.
But it was up to each member of my team to sell their wins to me.

THE OPPORTUNITY TO SPEND MORE TIME WITH THEIR KIDS, GET THINGS DONE AROUND THE HOUSE, AND TAKE CARE OF THEMSELVES

My product manager needed to have his gallbladder removed. Less than a week after his surgery, his step-father passed away. My developer needed to get his wisdom teeth pulled. He also needed to take his car in and to take his 6-month-old daughter to the doctor (yet again) to locate the source of her allergy-based eczema. And when the temperatures in Chicago hit record lows, a pipe burst in his home.

*This...**this is life**!* These are things that happen. And work, ugh! We make work so rigid when it needs to be flexible. It needs to move with our lives, not stand in front of us like a giant wall. It needs to flow with when we can work, and also, where we can work. Do we really need to be in the office to respond to email?

In the same breath, note I am not the biggest fan of fully remote work environments — at least not for me, personally. I feel there's still something magical when you can get a team of people together, in the same place, working on the same project. But on the 2-week break, we let people work from home so they can take care of their families and themselves. The standard 9-5, 5 days a week model doesn't give people time to do this.

I have two employees with children. And much like a customer journey in marketing, I wanted to understand more about the employee journey. To see what their schedule looked like.

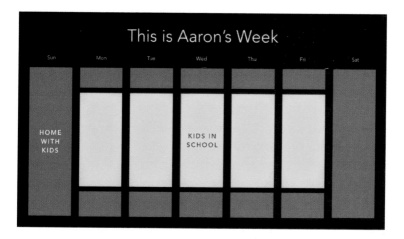

Take a look at Aaron's week. The only time he would have to himself is during the workday, when the kids are at school. And while I've only babysat my niece and nephew overnight, that's all a person needs to know kids are exhausting!

But still, bosses (who are parents themselves) ask employees (who are also parents) to:

• Dedicate themselves to their job all week
• Stay late to get the work done if needed
• Go home after work to take care of themselves
• Spend time with their families
• Seek downtime for themselves

Let's forget everything else that comes along with being an adult, raising a child, owning a home and car, taking care of extended family, friends, pets, eating right, working out, so on and so on.

Yet, we expect people to do all of this, over the course of a 2-day weekend, then demand they to come back to work refreshed and ready to go Monday morning? Are you shitting me?!!

But *wait*, it gets better!
Because **then** we expect it to happen week...
after week...
after week...
after week.

When people can schedule, when they can plan, I believe they're more empowered to take control of their lives.

03

How to use
6-Week Cycles

"Take a small step. Improve. Take
more small steps. Improve."

Much like meditation, 6-Week Cycles aren't something you jump right into and master. You start, with small steps.

Take a small step.
Improve.
Take more small steps.
Improve.

You'll see improvements as you examine and refine the process for your situation.

The goal is not to have a perfect 6-Week Cycle where everything goes according to plan. Instead, it's about having a process in place which allows for responsibility, flexibility, and the human element. It's a practice which starts by taking control over just a few hours per day.

While from the outside this methodology is similar to Agile, Jason Fried stressed cycles are not a sprint — so don't call them sprints. It is not about everybody going 110% for six weeks. It's about a controlled pace. We can do this by planning for the unknown and gradually cutting that time down until we can plan more for the known. Keep a strong focus on key tasks to be completed with the resources you have available.

When I've told people about this concept, their first question is, "do you work all 7 days during those 6-weeks?"

And, *what?!* No. No!
Absolutely not. That's insane.

We work 5 days per week, like everybody else. We make up the 2 weeks of time in between by being more productive during those 6-weeks, because we are focused on the work and preparation necessary to maximize efficiency; while still giving people room to live life.

The following chapters will show you how we do that. Starting with a 2-week planning session, we'll go through all of the steps involved with implementing this methodology.

	Week 1 (5/22 - 5/26)	Week 2 (5/29 - 6/2)	Week 3 (6/5 - 6/9)	Week 4 (6/12 - 6/16)	Week 5 (6/19 - 6/23)	Week 6 (6/26 - 6/30)
	Focus	Focus	Focus	Focus	Focus	Focus
You						
Monday						
Tuesday						
Wednesday						
Thursday						
Friday						
Developer						
Monday						
Tuesday						
Wednesday						
Thursday						
Friday						
Designer						
Monday						
Tuesday						
Wednesday						
Thursday						
Friday						

TL;DR

Want to skip the rest of the book? Here you go. This is the process. To learn more about each step, well, you're going to have to keep reading.

• Name your cycle
• List all of your tasks
• Setup each week at the top of the overview sheet
• Setup each day on individual weekly sheets
• Grey out any days employees are off or taking half days
• Fill in the overview sheet with each day's focus (that one thing the person absolutely needs to get done)
• Go through each week and write down the tasks required for each day

- Rearrange items, based on priority, until you have accounted for 6 or fewer hours per day
- Plan some kind of celebration for the last day of the cycle

04

List out everything you need to do

"We plan for flexibility.
We plan for breaks."

Get some whiteboards, large pads of paper, or even just a to-do list application and start writing out all of the items you need to complete. Begin with top-level categories/projects and list the tasks associated with each one.

By the time you're done, you should have conference room walls filled with everything in your heads.

For me, it is essential to have the tasks listed physically in front of me. I lose the concept of scale when I only look at things in a digital environment. To get everything out of my head, I lock myself inside the whiteboard room at WeWork. For about four hours, it's just me, Kanye, and some dry erase markers.

Name your cycles

I have this strange habit of naming my years in advance. It started over 5 years ago, when I made a list of the things I wanted to do over the next year. They weren't big things, just small things that made me happy. Like scoring a goal in hockey, writing a new song, or going on a boat.

It's rooted in the concept that we have the opportunity to write our own future; something that correlated back to cycles.

A friend who worked at Basecamp told me they named each cycle after different wars. Being on a big Hamilton kick at the time, the idea of going with US Presidents sounded fun. Working for a digital product company in the tourism sector, we changed cycle names to reflect different cities around the world. In 2019 we have Reykjavik, Calgary, Shanghai, Marrakesh, Orlando, and Moscow.

This concept played further into the product as we began to update our login screen image with a picture of a different city every time we updated the software. Since we push software updates at the end of every cycle, the image would always correspond with that cycle's city.

So name your cycle. Give it some personality, give it some flair! Pick names that have some meaning to you and your organization.

How to do a brain dump

1. Read all instructions before beginning

2. Select my *Kanyeness* playlist from Spotify

3. List the major categories of all active projects — this could be anywhere from 2 to 20 categories. It all depends on how many things you're trying to work on.

4. List all of the tasks to be completed under each category

5. Decide which items *you* need to complete. Anything which can be completed by someone else should be moved to a separate list and assigned to that individual.

6. Write down how long each task will take to complete. Any task longer than 90 minutes should be broken into smaller tasks.

7. Celebrate your dump with some kind of reward, because that...yeah, especially for your first one, was a lot of work.

One of the many, many things I feel like I did incorrectly when running my agency was expecting each person to do their job. It seemed like a real simple formula in my head. If I hire a person who can do web development, they should do web development. But it doesn't work like that.

I saw them as being independent. However, I feel as their leader, I needed to see them as extensions of myself. That it wasn't "what can they do" vs "what can I do". It needed to be, "I need to do this, and I get it done by having this person work on *X*."

But I needed to take responsibility for the tasks, not rely on someone else to figure it out. As a manager, it was my job to make sure my team had all of the tools and resources they needed to do their job. Including an understanding of exactly what they needed to do. I didn't necessarily need to know how they did it — that's why I hire specialists; but I needed to know the exact outcome expected.

As you go into your brain dump, keep in mind that:
- It's going to feel overwhelming
- They don't need to be in any particular order. You're just looking to get it all out of your head.
- Plan for one full day of brain dumping.
- Allow a few days to continue adding to the list. Even in that first four hours, you won't get everything out of your head. Random tasks are going to continue to pop up over the next few days. It's your job to capture those tasks like Pokémon.

Prepare your cycle sheet

In preparing for the next cycle, we need to first know each person's obligations. "Life" will always get in the way, but this is why we **plan** for flexibility. We plan for breaks.

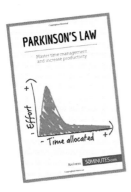

" work expands so as to fill the time available for its completion"

We refer to Parkinson's Law to understand a task is going to take the amount of time we allow for it.

And dammit, we *know* this already! We've done this since we were in school. Remember when you were given 2 weeks to complete an assignment, but you were able to complete it in 6 hours the night before it was due?!

With the cycle sheets, look ahead and block off any days someone is out or unavailable. Also note any big events which may prevent you, or someone else, from performing their best that day.

Work around these blocked days. Can an employee work 4 ten-hour days one week to have a day off? What's their workload like? Are they waiting on others before they can move on? There's no black & white here, it's all gray. Each employee's schedule is a case by case basis, and should be based on the question "How can we work around your schedule, and complete all of our tasks?"

How to prepare your cycle sheet

1. Ask each person to look at their calendars. Is there anything in their life that may interfere with their ability to perform their job in the next six weeks.
2. On the overview sheet, make those days gray and look to plan around them.

If a person requests too many days and it continually interferes with their ability to perform their work, you have a problem with that person not being able to do their job. Time is not the metric, we're looking at performance in this new results-oriented world you've embarked upon by reading this book.

List important milestones

Document any milestones necessary for project completion. On the overview sheet, each available date has a cell to list your focus. Concentrate on the one thing that needs to get done each day to help move the organization forward that cycle. You can add smaller, more specific tasks onto each day, but the overall focus for each day should account for a singular focus.

Each major task or milestone will have subsequent tasks attached to it. Continue to populate the overview sheet by adding the most important task that needs to be completed each day throughout the cycle.

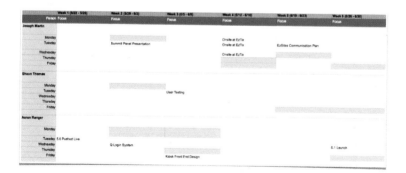

How to plan for tasks

1. List any major tasks or milestones on your sheet
2. Review with team members
3. Place those milestones and tasks onto the overview sheet

Plan in spreadsheets, not on your calendar?

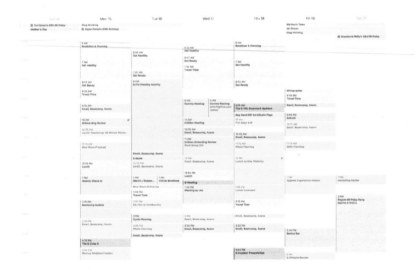

We found tasks move too much to be on a calendar. In a calendar, you're forced to plan items for a particular time, weeks in advance, allowing for very little flexibility. Having one or two things planned for your day, that works. You can work around those. But trying to plan how you're going to spend every hour of your day, every day of a week, for weeks in advance — life gets in the way. Too many things come up.

When we tried to plan it all on a calendar, it felt like a collapsing waterfall. If one thing went wrong, it messed up everything else. Plan in a spreadsheet instead, and you can easily track hours, as well as move things between days based on the number of hours required.

IF YOU FALL BEHIND
Move the task to a different day in the cycle, or look to shorten the amount of work required to complete the task.

With the cycle sheets, you can easily move tasks to a different week without messing up someone's day. In sharing the sheets with your team, people can also request time for a meeting without requesting a specific time. A manager can access an employee's sheet, see what items they have that week, and look to plan for a day that works best.

The spreadsheet also helps review hours before they happen. A lot of time tracking programs are rooted in the idea of tracking your time *after* it has passed. With 6-week cycles, you're more concerned about planning your time before the task occurs. Again, using Parkinson's Law to keep you in line.

With the spreadsheet, you can divide your hours between different projects and calculate totals in the right column. Things you don't complete each week get moved into a future week or removed from the cycle sheet completely with notes about why it was removed. Those notes should then be reviewed at the end of a cycle. Especially since, sometimes, we plan for the wrong things and don't realize it until it's too late.

05

The "And Then...?" Game

"Humans are awful at
estimating time."

I struggled with both prioritization and planning. My inability to plan or prioritize led to my team's inability to plan or prioritize. It's a waterfall effect.

I was not a good leader. If I was habitually late for every meeting, how could I expect my team to be on time for a meeting?

As you write down your major tasks, you're writing your wins. You plan to complete the tasks that make you a badass at your job. You also want to ensure there's an understanding of how to complete each major task before the cycle begins.

We messed up soooo many cycles planning to "plan a project" within a cycle. Only to find we had vastly underestimated the time & effort we needed to invest in the project's completion. Which, would ruin the meticulous planning we had done for the cycle. In turn, upsetting the team, and making us think cycles were stupid and never going to work for us.

But! We persevered. I really wanted this 6-on/2-off life. I'd push my team to examine where we went wrong and note what we needed to do differently for the next cycle — now that we had just shit all over this one.

Humans are awful at estimating time. Often it's because we omit the smaller steps involved in completing a task. Or, we simply haven't taken the time to define the subtasks involved in our larger tasks.

Indeed, there's a lesson to be learned from the 2000 cult classic movie, *Dude, Where's My Car?* While placing an order at a local fast food chain, Ashton Kutcher's character is continually asked *"and then?"* at the end of each item he requests. After repeating his order multiple times, his frustration grows. When the attendant asks, "and then?" again, he responds with, "and then you can put it in a brown paper bag."

And *that*! **That's** what we're looking for. It's this minute level of detail we're looking to achieve.

As you go through your tasks, push yourself to define them further.

While I'm not placing a food order, let's use the example of writing a blog article. I could easily put this on my list as "Blog Article — 1.5hrs." And I'm a decent writer, it shouldn't take me 90 minutes to write an article. Pffft! *C'mon*! I can knock that out. I wrote a book, dammit!

But, by asking "and then" I'm forced to play through that task further.

I need to write an article
....and then? I probably need to spend some time finding images to put in the article
....and then? I should ask someone to proofread it
....and theen? I need to get it ready to post online
...and theeen? I'll want to get it posted on our social media networks and in our newsletter
....and theeeen?

Now, I have some additional tasks to add to my sheet which help me better understand how much time I really need to spend on this task.

There's a really great side effect to this approach as well. It's subtle, and you may not have noticed it, but when I listed "*I should ask someone to proofread it*" I was helping someone else plan their time.

Meaning, when I put this task in my overview sheet, I can also request one of my team to include time in their calendar to proofread the article for me. When you start planning your time in advance, you encourage those around you to do the same.

The Power of Visualization

Something amazing happens when you plan. You're forced to visualize. Like an Olympic swimmer about to jump in the water, you're taking the time to run through the race. Instead of just letting the day happen to you, take control of it. If you need a meeting with another team member, contact them that morning to find a time that works.

Take time to go through the day in your mind.
Play it out.
Know what you need to do and when to do it.

I'll sometimes coordinate a playlist with a specific task. LotR (Fellowship of the Ring) soundtrack is my ultra focus playlist; it makes work an adventure to destroy evil. While on the other side, Kanye is my "at the whiteboard" playlist to help boost some confidence and get me excited about what I have coming up.

Playing through your day in advance allows you to anticipate potential roadblocks. It lets you go through the process before you jump into the work. And this, *c'mon*! We **know** this helps productivity. So in addition to the benefits of planning, visualization has been proven to help people complete tasks faster.

Having each team member plan their 6-Week Cycle also takes them through this process of visualization. Before each cycle begins, your management team should review the overview sheet and make modifications where necessary. As a group, walk through what needs to happen each week to try and identify any issues. It's almost like a group reading before you head off to the live performance. From the business side though, it helps you mitigate risks and minimize interruptions.

06

Plan for each day

" 'Too much stuff comes up, we can't plan ahead' is not a feasible excuse."

"Every minute you spend in planning saves 10 minutes in execution; this gives you a 1,000 percent return on energy."

- Brian Tracy, Training & Development Consultant

Since you know the focus of each day, list out the tasks associated with it. You can also start to place in time for tasks that aren't primary tasks.

Use the tabs at the bottom of the planning sheet to go through each day. By letting each employee plan their own day, you're also giving them the opportunity to know when they will be the most productive on the given task.

For each day, group everything into one of three categories.
• Planning
• Communicating
• Doing

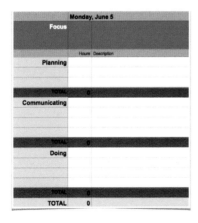

Planning time

Planning time is reserved for any task that requires your brain, a piece of paper and/or a calendar. Planning time is spent alone and may include interactions with other people to get questions answered.

Every day my team is encouraged to spend the first 30 minutes planning. To write out anything they need to get done that day, personal or professional. A brain dump. Every day. Because every day, something new happens to us. It requires us to make constant corrections to stay on course.

By listing these tasks in the spreadsheet:
· It tallies the amount of time spent per major category
· It allows the flexibility to place these items in your calendar each day based on the time you have available

Use this 30 minutes of daily planning to build your calendar for the day. Look at each task listed and create the same task in your calendar for the same amount of time.

PLANNING FOR TRAVEL TIME

We could easily say that travel to and from work does not need to be accounted for — but what if it could? Are there ways you can use this time towards something work related?

For some people, driving time is "their time". It's the only moment of peace they get to be by themselves, and the last thing they want to think about is work.

But that was a different world. First, you weren't being judged on results previously, only by time spent in the office. Second, you're going to have more time for yourself on the upcoming 2-week break. The car ride will no longer be the only salvation.

Look to get more out of travel times, maybe even planning yourself phone conferences during travel time. Microphones have gotten significantly better over the years, it's not like it used to be when people would take conference calls in the car and all you heard was the world around them.

And be careful out there driving! If you find it difficult to drive and talk, then don't do it. Stick with some music or talk radio. I know how tempting it can be to pull out your phone to send a quick text, or jot down a quick note. Just...don't do it. Utilize voice assisted applications if you need it do something.

Communication time

Perhaps the most vastly underestimated and unaccounted for part of most days. Communicating includes any time spent interacting with other people or responding to requests.

This includes:
• Replying to messages in project management applications like Base-camp or Asana
• Going through emails
• Any meetings — in-person or virtual
• Responding to client requests in forums or support-based applications

- Working with a business advisor
- Office hours
- Client check-ins

Anything that involves interacting with another person should be grouped under communicating. Warning — trying to get this area under control is one of most complex tasks you'll embark upon. It is also crucial to effectively managing the rest of your day.

Similar to "doing" time, you want to limit distractions while you're completing tasks. That includes scheduling time to check email, and closing your email program when you're not using it.

Time reserved to check email should be reserved for exactly that — checking email. When you're not checking email, quit your email program. Seriously, turn it off. It's so incredibly distracting.

A lot of people, myself included, have this terrible habit of constantly checking emails so we can feel productive. That when we get through emails quickly, we end up with a false sense of accomplishment.

Be productive.
Not distracted.

Set aside time to go through emails and treat it like a task.

I could absolutely go into an entire chapter about the benefits of shutting off distractions, but c'mon! We know we're going to be more productive when we only work on one thing. We can agree on that, right? Trying to bounce between a bunch of things is like being the jack of all trades and master of none.

So, I'd like to make a quick, crazy suggestion.

Start blocking out time for things like email and Slack. *Try*, just try checking it at 10am for an hour, and again at 2pm for 30-45minutes. Ideally, come into the office and keep email closed for the first part. Instead, knock out that first big task, THEN go into your email and project management tools, that will hijack your day. At this point, at least you'll have the first big task accomplished.

1 Distraction = 25 Minutes

According to a UC Irvine study, a person needs an average of 25 minutes to get back to the point they were before being distracted. Now I'm with you — it sounds like a lot. Plus we don't know who funded the study, so there are a whole lot of problems here with this number.

However, can we agree that a distraction does pull you away from what you were doing, and it then takes you *X* amount of time to catch up again? So, even without the 25 minutes, a distraction does impact our productivity. If we could limit the number of distractions per day, we would see some kind of exponential increase in productivity.

Distractions appear in all kinds of ways.
• Instant messages (Slack)
• A person stopping by your desk
• A call or text message
• A new email notification
• Someone burning popcorn in the kitchen

For argument's sake, let's say two distractions in one day could cost you up to an hour in productivity. In a time-based work environment, we don't care. We have nowhere to be until 5pm, when we're allowed to leave.

In a results-oriented environment, two distractions could be the difference between finishing your work day at 4pm or being done at 5pm. The longer you allow a task to take, the less time you have to do the things you care about in life.

As you go through work tomorrow, try to be cognizant of how many times you get distracted. Get a piece of paper and tear it in half every time you've been distracted. When you're finished, realize that three pieces of paper could equal one hour of your life.

Slack: The ultimate distractor

In August 2013 a program called Slack hit the market. In its simplest form, it's AOL Instant Messenger...for offices. They touted it as a way to cut down on email. Instead of waiting for responses, get answers in real time from your team.
It sounds great, they marketed it beautifully — but I feel there is a hidden flaw.

In a May 2018 article from TechCrunch, it's reported that Slack has 8 million daily active users. 8 MILLION PEOPLE getting distracted every day.

On top of it being a consistent source of distractions, I have some other concerns with it.

I'M AFRAID IT CREATES A "RIGHT NOW" CULTURE

Applications train humans how to use them. With Slack, it trains you to reach out to people who are online by showing whether they are available. This sets an expectation. If I reach out to someone who also has the application open, I expect to have my question answered immediately.

CREATES A DEPENDENCY ON ASKING QUESTIONS
INSTEAD OF LOOKING FOR ANSWERS

If anyone has ever messaged you on Slack, only to send you another message 5 minutes later saying, "nevermind", you'll know exactly what I'm talking about. It makes "messaging" the easiest way to get answers. Which, it is! 100%. However, the tradeoff for such a thing is having your own staff essentially serve as a support team to your own staff.

If you want to pay your staff to also handle remedial tasks, you can go right ahead. I would much rather keep my most productive members focused in the areas they're best at and enjoy doing the most.

KEEPS YOU CONSISTENTLY CONNECTED —
THIS CANNOT BE A GOOD THING!

The whole idea of working for 6 weeks and taking off for 2 weeks is to create breathing room among the team and individuals. The same stands with each day. We don't want to be exhausted with work each day during the cycle. It should exist in addition to our life, not *as* our life.

If you currently use Slack with your team, look to start setting parameters for usage. Encourage employees to turn off Slack during the day to focus on larger tasks and see if you can setup specific #emergency channels to prevent over-communication after hours.

Doing Time

After you've accounted for planning and communication time, you can place your tasks into daily plans. The doing tasks are for items that you will work on by yourself.

To do this, take your 90 minute items (or less, none larger than 90-minutes though) from your brain dump, and drop them into the doing area on daily sheets.

Try to align your tasks with the focus you've already listed for each day. Don't worry too much about getting it perfect the first time, it doesn't work that way. There's a 2 week break for planning because you're going to rearrange things multiple times as you look ahead.

Changes will also occur when you run the proposed cycle by a boss. Always start by planning for the biggest items first and trickling down from there.

Plan for 6-hrs per day

As you place time in each day for planning and communication, you may be shocked to see how little time you have for doing. If it feels like the days are running away from you and you can't get much done, this could be why.

For a typical 8-hr work day, we plan for 6-hrs of tasks. This includes our planning, breaks, and projects. A hyper-planned 6-hr day should break down into:

30 minutes of planning

+ 5.5-hrs of email, meetings, and tasks

+ 4 breaks at 15 minutes per break

+ 1 lunch at 60 minutes

————————————

= Your 8-hr Workday

When we first brought 6-wk cycles into the Canadian-based company that acquired my team, we had the chance to examine their Engineer's schedule. What was commonly thought of as 40 hours available per week quickly showed 15 actual hours available. Between communicating with internal stakeholders, ensuring his team had what they needed, and some regularly scheduled maintenance time, we found he only had a fraction of time available for hands-on development work.

The idea that, "too much stuff comes up, we can't plan ahead" is not a feasible excuse. And dammit! Too many people use this an excuse to not plan because they think it's too hard. In reality, we just need to plan for stuff to come up.

By planning for 6hrs/per day, each person has 2hrs of flexible time, if needed. Though we don't want to, we can cut into breaks and lunch time should we find tasks running over and we need to work harder that week.

If that's not enough, plan for two hours of time per day allocated to tasks that you are unable to predict.

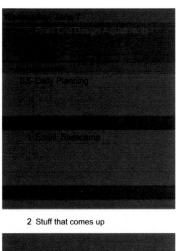

2 Stuff that comes up

As you build your next cycle sheet, look to reduce this number. Can you take it down to 1.5hrs next cycle? 1hr the cycle after that? Continue doing this until you can get those tasks inline, or in a more predictable state. It's that same practice of meditation I mentioned earlier. 6-week cycles are a practice.

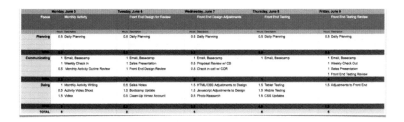

Focus	Monday, June 5 Monthly Activity	Tuesday, June 6 Front End Design for Review	Wednesday, June 7 Front End Design Adjustments	Thursday, June 8 Front End Testing	Friday, June 9 Front End Testing Review
Planning	0.5 Daily Planning	0.5 Daily Planning	0.5 Daily Planning	0.5 Daily Planning	0.5 Daily Planning
Communicating	1 Email, Basecamp 1 Weekly Check In 0.5 Monthly Activity Outline Review	1 Email, Basecamp 1 Sales Presentation 1 Front End Design Review	1 Email, Basecamp 0.5 Proposal Review w/ CS 0.5 Check in call w/ CCR	1 Email, Basecamp	1 Email, Basecamp 1 Weekly Check Out 1 Sales Presentation 1 Front End Testing Review
Doing	1 Monthly Activity Writing 0.5 Activity Video Shoot 1.5 Video	0.5 Sales Notes 1.5 Bootcamp Update 0.5 Clean-Up Vimeo Account	1.5 HTML/CSS Adjustments to Design 1.5 Javascript Adjustments to Design 0.5 Photo Research	1.5 Tablet Testing 1.5 Mobile Testing 1.5 CSS Updates	1.5 Adjustments to Front End
TOTAL	6	6	6	6	6

After you've completed one week, move onto the next one. In your mind, continue to run through your tasks in chronological order.

Covey's Time Management Matrix

If you are familiar with this already, cool! Like some kind of businessey, Choose-Your-Own-Adventure, jump ahead.

If you haven't, it's pretty slick. Covey did well to simplify tasks creating 4 categories:

• Urgent & important
• Not urgent & important
• Not important but urgent
• Not important and not really urgent either

The idea is that all tasks should fall into one of these 4 categories. To be the most effective with your time, you want to operate in zone 2. Completing tasks that are important to the organization but not urgent.

In zone 1, you should have been planning better. In zone 3, you really need take a step back and find out why you're even working on something if it's not important. In zone 4..."what is it you say you actually do here?"

COVEY'S TIME MANAGEMENT MATRIX

	Urgent	Not Urgent
Important	1	2
Not Important	3	4

Too many times, however, we're stuck in zone 1. Or worse, finishing a workday, only to realize we were in zone 3 the whole time. Understanding why you're completing the tasks, and their priority is crucial to being effective over the course of a 6-Week Cycle.

07

Check-in &
check-out meetings

"It's relaxed. It's personal. There's
nothing to prepare. Each person
gets chance to be heard."

Monday check-in meeting

Every Monday, on cycle only, we have afternoon meetings to review the upcoming week. Each person is responsible for making adjustments to their schedule if things change. Examine all changes, discuss blocked items, and ensure all meetings are scheduled.

And this will change as the week goes on.
It always does.

We've had it change the second we get out of a meeting. But! At least there is a plan in place, something we can measure. Something we can now start tracking to understand how often tasks are not getting completed. Which hopefully helps us to do better next time around.

How to run a check-in meeting:

1. Each person shares their weekly agenda
2. Coordinate and schedule any required meetings/reviews
3. Ask what problems could occur that week
4. Ask the team what tasks are important for management to focus on
5. Review improvements from the previous week

Friday check-out meeting

Every Friday, on cycle only, have an afternoon to review how things went the past week. Spend 2 minutes in silence to write down everything that went well and share it with the group. We also try to share something personal that went well that week.

This has become our favorite meeting. One of our team members, who works in South Africa that we've never personally met said, "I look forward to meetings, which isn't something people normally say."

It's relaxed.
It's personal.
There's nothing to prepare.
Each person gets their chance to be heard.

And as the leader, I get the chance to hear the most important things happening to each person on my team. They also have direct access to me. Every week.

If you were to start with just one piece of action from this book, I highly recommend this. If nothing else, at least implement these meetings with your team. I truly can't believe the impact they've had on my team.

How to run a check-out meeting:
1. 2 mins in silence writing down what went well that week
2. Each person shares what went well
3. 2 mins in silence writing down what did not go well that week

4. Each person shares what didn't go well

5. As a group discuss how to improve things for the next week

Be Consistent

In Chicago, we have two different train systems. The "el" primarily travels around Chicago picking passengers up every 5-15 minutes. The Metra stretches out further from the city and into the surrounding suburbs. Different from the el, Metra runs methodically and focuses on consistent pickup times.

Part of that consistency comes from their ability to make up time by moving faster. The same way we can't expect to run our employees at top speed, all the time — Metra cannot maintain a consistent schedule if they operate their trains at full speed, all the time. They'd lose their consistency with the slightest mix-ups.

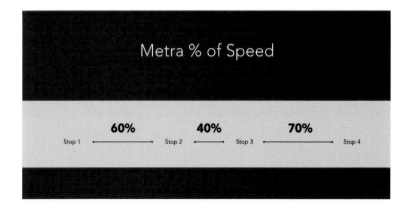

Instead, they run the trains at 60% or 70% of their speed, knowing they can go up to 80% if they need to; 100% if really desperate.

In this same idea, we shouldn't look to cram each person's cycle where they're expected to give 100% every day. We should look to run our teams at the rate that gets us the best consistency and results, not which garners the most amount of time.

End of Cycle Celebration

In Charles Duhigg's "The Power of Habit" he talks about a simple formula for reprogramming better habits in humans. He breaks bad habits down into three steps:

1) the trigger — this causes you to take the action

2) the action — the thing you do because of the trigger

3) the reward — the emotional or physical benefit of the action

Using this same method, he stresses that we can reprogram our brains into good habits by identifying the trigger, changing the action, and facilitating a reward. We've tried to incorporate this idea of reinforcement through reward by establishing an end of cycle celebration.

During the cycle planning phase, appoint a team member to be in charge of the celebration. Give them a budget and time within the upcoming cycle to plan the event. We generally plan ours for the last Friday in week six. These end of cycle celebrations serve as the reward element to Duhigg's equation. Something that supports the action of working for six weeks with a reward.

My team has gone to Blackhawks games, escape rooms, and comedy shows. By selecting a different person to plan the celebration each cycle, everyone gets a chance to experience something new, keeping the end of cycle celebrations fun and different every time.

GIVE RECOGNITION AT THE END OF EACH WEEK AND CYCLE

People like to be celebrated — right? I'm not crazy on this one. We all appreciate recognition for the work we've done. And when we can create the routine of celebrating an individual's accomplishments, we give them something to look forward to.

If you don't have superiors, find a mastermind or peer group to help you celebrate your wins.

08

Cycle Sheet Extras

"The idea is that these items can be quickly (hopefully!) talked about, and may even help understand what/why scheduling got off track in a particular week."

QUOTES COLUMN:

Reserve a place in your cycle sheets for quotes. Use this list to jot down any:

• Praise from a customer
• Negative comments or feedback
• Something we heard or read from a competitor
• Funny things people wrote in an email or posted to Slack
• Things that weren't meant to be funny that someone wrote in an email or posted on Slack

Place those quotes into your cycle sheet and bring them up on a check out call as well.

ITEMS TO DISCUSS:

This column is the chance to jot down any quick notes for things to talk about with the team during a check-in or check-out meeting. It can include current project questions, new ideas, or anything else that has come up that week.

The idea is that these items can be quickly (hopefully!) talked about, and may even help understand what/why scheduling got off track in a particular week. Going back through the sheet at the end of the cycle, review this list to see which items you need to accommodate for next time.

GOALS:

If you have any smaller goals to try and accomplish that week, you have this area available. These can be goals for one person, for the team, or an organization.

TASK LIST:

The task list is a place to dump ideas you want to revisit.

Always be planning

During a cycle, have the next cycle's sheet ready with the overview and weekly sheets available. This allows you to quickly place items into an upcoming cycle as they come up.

If you know there is a scheduled meeting — jump ahead and put time into the next cycle sheet now. If it's a large meeting, mark it as the focus for that day to ensure you plan around it when you get to that cycle.

For me, a big part of organization is having a place to put things. I read about this approach with children years ago. How, if a child knows exactly where they need to put something, they're more likely to clean up their toys. If a place is not specifically assigned for that item, they are less likely to put that toy away.

This...this just made sense! And if it's easy enough for a child, it should be easy enough for me to accomplish in a hurry when I'm trying to quickly move through things.

In having upcoming cycle sheets at the ready, you have a place to put things. Ideas, concepts, discussions or future meetings that are needed. You'll be in a constant state of forward thinking by having future sheets available.

09

A Keystone Habit

"What would happen if my team made planning our singular focus."

In the same "The Power of Habit" book by Charles Duhigg, he also tells the story of Alcoa Metal's CEO, Paul O'Neill. In it, he reinforces the idea of having a singular focus. For Alcoa Metals, he tells of their focus on safety and how it led to a better work environment with increased profits. With 6-week cycles, I wanted to see what would happen if my team made planning our singular focus.

What if that was the one thing we tried to do best?!
Who would we be?
What would be possible if we mastered planning?!

6-week cycles became our keystone habit. With it we found a better culture, increased productivity, and the ability to hit project deadlines.

I think a big part of it was luck for us. We're lucky enough to have the kind of work that allows us to operate this way and a nimble team that was able to handle the challenge.

This is why I don't believe 6-week cycles are the answer for all organizations, but it is a staring point. The chance to start a conversation around employee happiness in any organization.

And yes, YES I wanted a full chapter for just this idea.
It's THAT important.

GO!

Go start a conversation at your company about employee happiness.

.0

6-week cycles are
not the answer

"It takes time and can only ever be
practiced — not perfected."

6-week cycles are not the magical solution your team has been looking for. This methodology is not meant to be followed line by line; truly, it's intended to start a conversation. A conversation about employee happiness within your organization, and honestly, one about your own damn happiness, too.

Your company doesn't need to use 6-week cycles, but you can. You can take the initiative to sit down with your boss and ask them to help you understand your responsibilities for the next two months.

You are entitled to this.
You have a right to know what work you have ahead of you.
Which, honestly, your boss may not be able to look that far ahead.

But you can. You can take the initiative to draw up your next 6 weeks and bring it to your boss for approval. Do the work for him/her. In the world of sales and marketing, it's this idea of "make it as easy as possible for the customer to say yes".

When you ask your boss to look ahead, it forces them to ask their bosses to look ahead. Which, may require sales people to look further ahead and set better expectations with clients. The same way we want to respect our own time, sales people and those who interact with clients need to respect the time of the company.

If your company is not happy with you trying to plan, or reprimands you for asking, look to leave. Any company that looks to hold you back from advancing in yourself, or your career, is a dinosaur. They deserve to go extinct. But when people absorb these kind of work environments, we allow these archaic practices to persist. Like people who complain about Spirit Airlines, but then still buy tickets because they're cheap. We're doing it to ourselves! Let's break that wheel. Dany will be proud.

But planning ahead... Knowing, just slightly, what your future holds — I genuinely believe you can do this.

You've read the book, now download the templates and figure it out for yourself. Dig up every reason it doesn't work for your team and let's talk about it. Join me at 6weekcycles.com and let's try to find a way it can.

The same way we heard an idea from Basecamp and ran with it, take our framework. Deconstruct it.

Make your own plan.
Bring it to your boss.
And then...prepare for it to be shit all over.

Which, don't be upset! I'm just trying to help set some expectations here. It's not going to work...at first. Adjust it, and try again.

We were ready to give up on this idea after the first cycle. Nothing went according to plan.

The second time we tried to run 6-week cycles — same damn thing.

The third time we tried was the most frustratingly comical mess. Especially with me being a cheerleader for the idea saying, "c'mon guys, third time's a charm!"

We were on the second day of the cycle when a project came in and wiped the entire plan for the cycle right out the door. Everything we had worked on was a waste. But! That happens with projects, all the time, all over the world. Get over it.

The whole time we were failing, we were still learning. Refining our method. We'd take note of what upset us and improve the process next time.

It was like filling the holes in a leaky boat. Every. damn. time. we fixed one thing, something else popped up. But that's....it's all part of it. It's a part of building an organization and a workforce from reactive to proactive.

Like meditation, be patient when bringing this idea into an organization. It takes time and can only ever be practiced — not perfected.

But! Be persistent.

Having this information is important. How are we supposed to look ahead in our own lives, or feel accomplished at the end of a work week when we don't even know what needs to get done?!

And that....that's all I've got.

Thanks for reading my book.

J. Martin

Joe Martin, Author

Resources

This book is intended to serve as a how-to for the methods I've instituted with my team. These aren't perfect, nor do they work for every organization. There are meant to serve as a starting to point to help an individual or organization get started with some of the ideas presented within this book.

You can access these resources online at 6weekcycles.com. You can also sign up for my 6-week cycle accountability course where you'll work with my team on implementing 6-week cycles within your own processes. We'll go step-by-step over the course of six weeks to help you improve your ability to effectively plan and answer any questions you have along the way.

I hope this helps you begin a new work methodology that helped change my life.

About the Author

Joe Martin has worked in the creative industry since 2001, gaining experience in design, marketing, and leadership. As a seasoned entrepreneur, he is passionate about building real-world communities and improving corporate culture.

In addition to Martin Creative and the Q, he is an active voice in Chicago. He has served as a judge & mentor for Google Startup Weekend events, worked with students through DePaul University's entrepreneurship program, and launched a networking group called The Entrepreneur's Workshop. His ideas on content and design have paved the way for international speaking opportunities. When he's not working, Joe plays competitive ice hockey, performs hip-hop songs on his acoustic, and travels to take food tours around the world.

He hopes this book serves as a shoulder for someone else to stand on. The same way he's been inspired to look at work, family, and community in a different way, he hopes it can ignite a spark in others to do the same.